contemporary Glamour

contemporary Glamour

opulent interiors from grand to exotic

Ali Hanan
with captions by Kate Dwyer

Photography by Deidi von Schaewen

MITCHELL BEAZLEY

First published in Great Britain in 2002 by Mitchell Beazley, an imprint of
Octopus Publishing Group Limited, 2–4 Heron Quays, London E14 4JP

Commissioning Editor: Emma Clegg
Executive Art Editor: Auberon Hedgecoe
Senior Editor: Lara Maiklem
Copy Editor: Lindsay Porter
Designer: Emily Wilkinson
Proofreader: Colette Campbell
Indexer: Hilary Bird
Location Researcher: Nadine Bazar
Production Controller: Angela Couchman

ISBN 1 84000 548 3

A CIP catalogue record for this book is available from the British Library

Typeset in Futura Book
Produced by Toppan Printing Co. (HK) Ltd.
Printed and bound in China

PREVIOUS PAGE Miami's South Beach is home to many Art Deco-style hotels built
in the 1930s and '40s. The Marlin, considered the "rock and roll" hotel of South
Beach, contains a popular recording studio and is frequented by many well-known
musicians. Barbara Hulanicki, The Marlin's interior designer, calls the style in the
lobby bar of the hotel – where every surface shimmers with silver – "Techno Deco".

RIGHT The Devi Garh Hotel in Rajasthan was originally a palatial 18-century fort. It
took two years for owner Lekha Poddar – whose Delhi home can be seen on pages
96–7 – and her team to strip the building, which was originally made up of 250
separate rooms. The hotel is now a minimal but luxurious sanctuary of white marble
accented by gold, black, and semi-precious stones.

INTRODUCTION

This book is your entry into the fantasy world that is Contemporary Glamour. It holds in its gloved hands the keys to the most alluring locations around the world. As you turn each page, allow yourself to step open-eyed into grand chateaux, luxurious five-star hotels, lavish homes, and breathtaking palaces.

Picture waking up in Pierre Cardin's Palais Bulles (Bubble Palace), a stunning house in the south of France made entirely of spheres connected by winding tunnels. Imagine floating starfish-style on the tranquil waters of a black marble pool at the Amanpuri Hotel in Phukhet, Thailand. Now travel to London and perch on Marilyn Monroe's luscious, ruby-red lips (the sofa that is, inspired by Salvador Dali) in London's swankiest hotel, The Sanderson.

Fantasy is about letting your imagination run riot. Why not indulge in make-believe? As your eyes feast on each page, allow yourself to dream about what it must be like to live in these fairytale places. Feel the cool texture of Italian marble floors beneath your feet. Luxuriate in a petal-strewn tub. Dream on beds in palaces.

Fantasy is the lifeblood of glamour. When it comes to literal definitions, "contemporary" bears no surprises. Its roots are in the Latin *com*, meaning together, and *temporarius*, or relating to time (from *tempus*, time). "Glamour", however, has extraordinary, mystical roots. The word originates from the 18th-century Scottish, "grammar": occult practices were associated with learning, so the word originally meant to cast a spell. Glamour, in other words, is pure magic.

Glamour has, like a sorcerer, continually reinvented itself. In its youth, glamour was bewitching. In its middle age, it became ostentatious. Periods of excess, like the Roaring Twenties and the Overdone Eighties, overdosed on the fake and flashy side of glamour. "Glam", its nickname, became a byword for trash. As it has aged, glamour has matured. In the Noughties, glamour became elegant and poised. Over time, experience has made it wise and beautiful.

In the 21st century, glamour no longer rests on its laurels or looks. Time has given it a depth of character. Glamour bows down before its history and draws inspiration from its ancestors, but, at the same time it looks forward, anticipating the future and reacting to the present moment. Look into glamour's crystal ball and you see it: past, present, and future at once.

PREVIOUS PAGE LEFT Stairs from Pierre Lombard's living room climb to a mezzanine-level bedroom crowned by a giant arch of glass bricks. The transparent bricks and enormous windows ensure that the house is bathed in light. Views over the African landscape are unrestricted.

PREVIOUS PAGE RIGHT Plenty of light, white walls, and plain wooden floors make up the backdrop for the splashes of red provided by the sculptural furniture in Laurent Buttazoni's Paris apartment, a former furniture factory. Red – Buttazoni's favourite colour – is repeated throughout the interior, which is simple with unusual accents such as the chunky crystal chandelier. Buttazoni designs elaborate sets for fashion designer John Galliano's shows. Jan Ekselius designed the undulating chaise and ottoman around 1970.

LEFT This boldly geometric house, where there are no 90-degree angles in the furniture or building, was designed by John Lautner in 1963 and has been used as a set for many a James Bond film. The interior of the house, which sits atop a cliff overlooking the city of Los Angeles, manages to be earthy even as it takes on futuristic forms. It has been constructed from natural materials like glass, wood, concrete, steel, and leather.

ABOVE There are no stairs in Pierre Cardin's Côte d'Azure house, Palais Bulles (Bubble Palace). Instead, the concrete pods that are rooms are linked by tunnel-like sloping corridors. The house was designed by Hungarian architect Antti Lovag – famous for his sphere constructions – in 1976 and was conceived as a "living human body" with joints and arteries. Pierre Cardin bought the house, still under construction, in the 1980s.

Peer closer. Different epochs and rooms come into view. The globe reveals the 1920s, where dining rooms were the must-have backdrop to a glamorous life: "one" displayed one's silver cutlery, crystal glasses, and embossed linen napkins. In the Swinging Sixties, the bedroom became the G-spot on the interior agenda, with beds shaped like love hearts, covered with hot pink satin sheets. Later, in the Sensual Seventies, living rooms with fur-lined conversation pits were fabulously de rigueur.

Rub the ball again to see the current view. You might be surprised: it's a bathroom. Throughout the 20th century, Hollywood celebrities tried to give the bathroom sex appeal: George Cukor's film, *The Women*, shows Joan Crawford lying in a chariot-style crystal bath set on a crest of gilded waves, making treacherous calls on her phone. Later came *The Seven Year Itch*, where Marilyn Monroe lies discreetly covered by a clouds of foam while a plumber repairs her taps.

Finally architects and designers gave the bathroom the kiss of life. Modern living demanded it as our lives became increasingly fast-paced. Taking time to soak in a hot tub is now a pure indulgence. As Dale Keller, designer and architect for Aman Hotels says, "now we want homes to be sanctuaries, which is why bathrooms are now as big in size – if not bigger – than bedrooms".

The crystal ball also reveals that contemporary glamour isn't just about rooms, or interiors. It's also about the people who create them. People have always animated glamour: Marlene Dietrich once famously said, "Glamour is what I sell, it is my stock in trade." Wherever she went she left a trail of stardust behind her. Even after all these years, her memory still sparkles, like the light perpetually reflected in Versailles' Hall of Mirrors.

Hollywood's leading lights are part of glamour's past. Like rooms, glamour has cast its light on a new set of illuminaries. Blame

ABOVE A futuristically shaped window in one of the two living rooms in Pierre Cardin's house looks out onto a pool that meets the horizon, giving the building a submarine-like quality. In other parts of the house porthole windows punctuate the smooth, curvilinear shells of the pod-like rooms made from steel frames sprayed with concrete. No specific plans were made for the building, which was constructed room by room.

French taste shaper, Philippe Starck, who, like a snake charmer, magnetized crowds with the cult of the celebrity designer. In the 1980s, a time when Madonna sang *Material Girl* in her conically cupped Jean Paul Gaultier dress, Starck began to put design and designers on show. His feminine, organic, enthralling interiors then (and now) put people on stage, and by doing so, they are cast – along with the creator – into the spotlight.

Take the Royalton Hotel in New York or the London hotels, The Sanderson and St Martin's Lane. To be seen and be part of the Starck scene is part of the attraction, but the furniture and furnishings are equal stars. Each hotel becomes a flagship store and gives the pieces – 35 one-eyed barstools in front of a back-lit onyx bar, gold chairs the shape of molars, garden gnomes that serve as tables – an iconic status. At St Martin's Lane Hotel, there is even "colour therapy". Guests create their own environments with interactive lights, altering the colours to match their moods. Of course it costs a fortune, but the attraction is the chance to play a lead role in Starck's stage show.

Following Starck's lead, the former "accountants" of the creative world are now *glitterati*. The glamour cognoscenti are now putting once-forgotten architects and designers back into the limelight. Pierre Cardin has revived Hungarian architect Antti Lovag's Palais Bulles, entrepreneur John Huggins has saved Charles Deaton's modernist opus, the Sculptured House, from wolves, and the Goldsteins have restored John Lautner's angular Los Angeles house to its former splendour.

In the wider world, fashionistas and starlets now vie for their attention. David Collins (responsible for Claridges' makeover) has become Madonna's muse; Frank Gehry (Bilbao Guggenheim, Vitra Design Museum) has designed Issey Miyake's New York store; and über-cool neo-modernist Rem Koolhaas (Las Vegas Guggenheim) has created an eye-popping store for Miuccia Prada in New York. Indeed, fashion and interior design have now dovetailed: many of the homes in this book belong to haute couture designers, including the likes of Pierre Cardin, Matthew Williamson, Mary McFadden, Didier Bohbot, Wolfgang Joop, and Thierry Mugler.

Glamour, like fashion, is constantly evolving. Traditional clichés of glamour – teardrop crystal chandeliers, starched linen doilies, and

RIGHT New York fashion designer Mary McFadden's apartment is an extravagant display of gold accented with black furnishings. Although the apartment makes strong references to the Byzantine period, with opulent gold leaf and stencilling copied from Byzantine churches, McFadden freely mixes furniture from different countries and historical periods. Furniture from Tibet, Japan, Korea, China, and South-East Asia is included in the apartment. The table seen here is a Chinese Tang altar and the candlesticks are from the Japanese Edo period (1605–1867).

fine hand-woven Persian rugs – are *so* passé. Contemporary glamour now reflects as many different styles of homes as there are people who own them. As architect Frank Lloyd Wright so succinctly said, "There should be as many kinds of house as there are kinds (styles) of people and as many different individuals."

While each home in this book is an entity in itself, the homes generally fall, like people, into character. The five chapters reveal glamour's five most outstanding traits and are divided to reflect its many faces. Glamour's sensibilities are intrinsically Indulgent, yet for others glamour is Timeless, Exotic, Sedate, or Eclectic.

Glamour's Indulgent sensibility satisfies its own desires. Indulgent follows Ilse Crawford's dictum in *The Sensual Home*, where, if "we allow ourselves to follow the yearnings of our hearts, and the messages conveyed by our senses, as well as the easily misled dictates of our supposedly rational minds" we will create an interior that satisfies our hearts' longings.

Timeless is glamour's immortal side. While sensibilities rebel against each other from one decade to the next, there are always pieces and places that transcend time and boundaries. Contemporary glamour mixes classics in its wardrobe. For glamour, certain looks and pieces never go out of style.

When glamour wants romance, it turns to Exotic. Whether it's an urban apartment filled with jewels from distant cultures or a former maharajah palace turned hotel, Exotic adores the allure of far-off lands – whether physical or purely in the imagination.

Sedate is the sensibility glamour turns to when it needs a haven. Sedate glamour provides a sanctuary for its inhabitants and its beauty is more than skin deep. Sedate is quiet, contemplative, and thoughtful.

Lastly, there is glamour's wild lovechild, Eclectic. It does whatever it wants. The only thing Eclectic believes in is its own taste. The people that shape these places are free thinkers, breaking all conventional rules.

It's time to indulge in a glamour fantasy and meet the owners and their houses. Can you hear the sound of keys turning in locks? *Contemporary Glamour* is about to cast its beguiling spell on you. As glamour's stardust settles, you, too, become part of all that glitters.

LEFT An elaborate Oriental lampshade hovers over a daybed laden with colourful bolsters and cushions in fashion designer Matthew Williamson's London bedroom. He has created a playful, bright atmosphere with a flamboyant use of colour and pattern. Bright "Schiaparelli shocking pink" – named after the surrealist 1930s fashion designer Elsa Schiaparelli – is used on the window frames and low table. Amarylis red is used with gusto and accented with fluorescent yellow.

INDULGENT

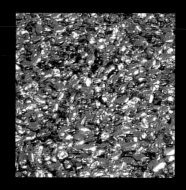

Indulgent glamour is dedicated to personal

pleasure. Indulgent taste, when applied to the

appetite, is purely epicurean. Indulgent homes are

no less sybaritic. Indulgent loves to please itself,

to give in to every whim and fancy.

Its heart's desires are all that matter.

The home-cum-gallery of art dealers Marianne and Pierre Nahon in the south of France houses extravagant pieces such as the glass table that encases delicate pieces of gold leaf by artist Yves Klein.

LEFT Chateau Notre Dames des Fleurs, a 19th-century Italian-style chateau, is home to the Nahon's gallery, Galerie Beaubourg, and is set in gardens decorated with works by the artists represented by the Nahons. Rustic rough stonework borders the organic curves of a pool in the garden.

ABOVE The Nahons' surreal table, a work by César, is supported by columns of flowing molten gold. It contrasts with the restrained lines of a modernist bookcase designed in the 1930s by Charlotte Perriand.

f Indulgent wants a room carpeted with gold-covered chocolates, it shall have one. If it likes to collect art, it shall turn its home into a gallery. Indulgent dares to follow its dreams. Indulgent is what we would all like to be if only we would allow ourselves the pleasure.

Indulgent has had its champions throughout history. Take Cleopatra, who loved to indulge her senses. While history still debates her beauty and reputation, her sensual pursuits remain legendary.

While Hollywood's Theda Bara, Claudette Colbert, and Elizabeth Taylor have added to her mystique, stories of her passion for drinking pearls dissolved in vinegar and scenting her barge sails with cedarwood have immortalized her. Indulgent applauds her seduction of Julius Caesar: she arrived to meet him on a barge with purple sails steered by silver oars while lying under a gold-embroidered awning dressed as Aphrodite. No wonder he was spellbound.

ABOVE The chunky, rounded shapes of the furniture and fireplace in the New York living room of fashion designer Wolfgang Joop reflect his penchant for late 1940s and early '50s design. The lamps, leopard print velvet chaise, and chenille sofa are all by French designer Jean Royère.

RIGHT Pale parquet flooring and the gold fireplace give the living room an air of polished glamour. The Polish high-society artist Tamara Lempicka painted the original *Girl With Teddy Bear* in the 1940s, while the '50s chairs flanking the fireplace are by French architect and furniture designer Jean Prouvé.

Indulgent also admires the excesses of Louis XIV, the Sun King, or as Andrée Putman more scathingly calls him, "Narcissus strolling around his Hall of Mirrors". For the Sun King, indulgence took the shape of glitzy, gaudy, material possessions – and the more the merrier. His court at Versailles matched his ego in size. Its sheer scale makes it as much a visual feast as its decoration. With Versailles' famed Hall of Mirrors, where 17 mirrors echo the 17 windows, the palace was (and still is) the prize on Indulgent's mantelpiece.

While Voltaire described Versailles as a "masterpiece of bad taste and magnificence", the Sun King's excesses live on, spilling over into contemporary interiors in the shimmer of Rachel Morris's pink and pearlescent stencilling, the Marlin Hotel's throne-like chairs, and

PREVIOUS PAGE Erika and Rolf Hoffman's Berlin home-cum-gallery contains this spectacular installation called *Untitled (Placebo – Landscape for Roni, 1993)* by the late artist Felix Gonzalez-Torres. The supply of 455kg (1,000lb) of gold cellophane-wrapped sweets is endlessly replenished.

ABOVE The tiles in this bathroom in the Nilaya Hermitage Hotel in Goa are reminiscent of work by quirky Spanish architect Gaudí – a new take on the traditional Indian tiled bathroom.

RIGHT Water falling into the pool at the Nilaya Hotel is echoed by the fluid curves of the bridge and the flowing fabric draped to form the canopy above.

ABOVE The interior of this cruiser, that island-hops in the Mediterranean Sea, was designed by interior architect and designer Frederic Mechiche to reflect the elegance of a 1930s English pleasure boat.

LEFT The pattern on the tables in the dining area of the boat is a work painted directly onto the surface by artist Jean François Migno. Light is subtly controlled by metal wall sconces in floating abstract shapes, designed by Mechiche.

NEXT PAGE The white leather ceiling in the Mechiche-designed boat is simple but luxurious. The horizontal lines of the blinds and hand-tufted carpet echo the nautical stripes on the hand-woven wool upholstery of the banquette seating.

Wolfgang Joop's tall, handsome candelabras. Indulgence, the impetus behind the masterpiece, dear Voltaire, is what makes it magnificent. Anyway – did Louis XIV care what Voltaire thought? He pleased himself. To him, that was all that mattered.

Where Cleopatra indulged her senses, and the Sun King indulged his every whim, Rachel Morris indulges in a more simple pleasure: bathing. Modern lives find less and less time for the luxury of a scented bath. In-out showers now suit our in-out lives. Rachel Morris has splashed out on an extravagantly large bathroom in her Northumberland home. "For me, lounging in the bath is pure decadence," she says. "As I bathe, I watch the light shimmer on a beaded curtain at the foot of the tub: it's so mesmerizing, rather like a disco ball." She advocates another "old-fashioned" bathroom staple –

ABOVE High-backed armchairs in the lobby of the Royalton Hotel create spaces
of intimacy in a very public environment. An enormous stretch of rich blue carpet,
edged with a pattern of ghosts, runs the full length of the lobby and reinforces
the feeling of grandeur and luxury.

RIGHT Opulent colours and low lighting combine with reflective and mirrored surfaces
to create an aura of moody glamour in the lobby bar of the Royalton Hotel.
The horn-like "Lucifer" wall sconces form a line along the wall of the lobby, echoing
the row of smooth, pebble-like bar stools – two of many pieces custom-designed
by French designer Philippe Starck. Mahogany walls line the 30-metre (100-foot)
length of the lobby. The hotel, which was opened in 1988, remains a place
of worship for Starck design fans.

ABOVE A dining table designed by John Barman, an interior designer, is surrounded by chairs that are delicate and glass-like despite the solidity of their design. They allow light to fill the entire room.

LEFT Curvilinear red vintage glass pieces complement red leather Barcelona chairs designed by Mies van der Rohe in 1929 and the reflective modular shapes of the screen in the background.

NEXT PAGE Refined modernist decoration is reflected in the bold shapes, reflective surfaces, and bright colour scheme in Barman's living room. A silver bubble screen by Verner Panton provides a stunning focal point. The smooth, shiny floor is poured concrete.

the dressing room. Once de rigueur in the early 20th century, today's world doesn't seem to have space for it – and more's the pity.

Indulgent likes to live with its great loves. For Marianne and Pierre Nahon, their love is art. Guests covet the contemporary pieces in their home-cum-gallery in the south of France. Almost everything in the house is like a sculpture, from the glass table filled with gold leaf to the Dali-esque lounge table. For Wolfgang Joop, his love is spotting soon-to-be collector's items, such as the work of 1950s designer Serge Mouille. (Joop bought these pieces long before Mouille was a twinkle in collectors' eyes).

Then, of course, there are the places Indulgent goes to on holiday. The Marlin Hotel, where the music cognoscenti (Grace Jones, Aerosmith, U2) congregate, on South Beach, Florida, is one such getaway. With its lustrous silver colour scheme, a guest can only expect to shimmer and shine. When in New York, Indulgent stays at the

Royalton Hotel, fashioned by celebrity designer Philippe Starck in 1988. When it was built, Starck added the two ingredients of glamour: excess and celebrity. Just as Versailles became the place to worship the Sun King, the Royalton Hotel became Starck's design Mecca.

Indulgent admires the work of Stark, which is design decadence. Take the famous squid-like alien lemon squeezer. "For me," he said, "it's more a symbolic micro sculpture than a functional object. Its real purpose is not to squeeze thousands of lemons but to enable a newlywed to engage in a conversation with his mother-in-law."

In other words, the product is a useless indulgence and no more. It has no practical qualities, except as a tool for social bonding. But that's what Indulgent cares so passionately about. As long as Indulgent has satisfied its desires, it is blissfully content. A room carpeted with chocolates? Just the thought seems so decadent.

ABOVE The futuristic lobby bar of The Marlin Hotel in Miami was designed by Barbara Hulanicki, founder of the Biba clothing line in London made popular in the 1960s by Twiggy, Brigitte Bardot, and Marianne Faithfull.

RIGHT All of the furniture in The Marlin Hotel was designed by Hulanicki. These chairs were inspired by jellyfish. The sensual shapes are complemented by smooth brushed-aluminium tabletops.

NEXT PAGE The Marlin was built in 1939 by architect L. Murray Dixon and refurbished by Barbara Hulanicki for the current owners in 1997. A shimmering aura is created with chairs covered in beige satin, sheer silver metallic curtains, and brushed-aluminium pillars.

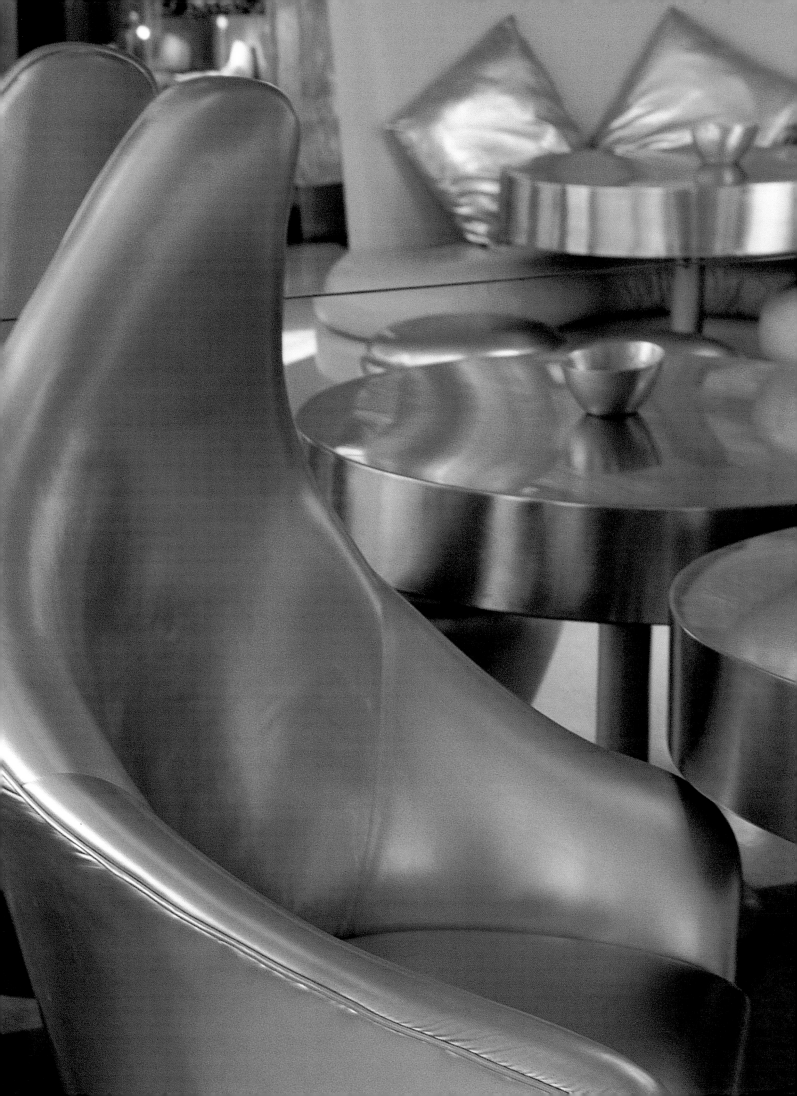

LEFT The Victorian-style bathroom in Rachel Morris' Northumberland home is brought up to date with a modern palette of pale lilac and white. A beaded curtain and glass chandelier provide a glamorous backdrop for the stand-alone cast-iron bath with gilded legs – the centrepiece of this indulgent and ultra-feminine space.

ABOVE The subtle damask stencils on this wall in Rachel Morris's house are from her own Stencil Library range and provide an elegant background for her romantic collection of intricately decorated frames, distressed gold letters, and baroque mantel clock.

Timeless glamour endures. Transcending trends,

it remains constant while fashions and sensibilities

shift like sand. Timeless is at the eye of the interior

design storm as tastes are tossed aside, upturned,

and abandoned. Faddish looks come and go,

but those that are classics live on and on and on.

PREVIOUS PAGE In Jacqueline Morabito's home in the south of France, a bas-relief of cherubs provides a dreamy bedhead with a delicately carved, distressed wooden chair acting as bedside table. The absence of colour focuses the eye on form and pattern.

LEFT Stripped-down classicism in the form of pale-coloured chandeliers and tableware is combined to contrast with modern pieces.

ABOVE The arrangement of ivory-handled hairbrushes on a table in the bathroom is both restful and elegant. All of the furniture, including the whimsical coat stand, was designed by Jacqueline Morabito.

Timeless has staying power. It isn't swayed by fashion's dictates. If a style transcends centuries and decades, it is Timeless – that is its criteria. Timeless style is immortal and, as Californian architect Frank Gehry says, it is what all interior design should strive for. "Architecture," he extolled, "should speak of its time and place, but yearn for timelessness."

Legendary interior design seer, Andrée Putman, agrees. She is famed for her ability to create classic designs – a quality that makes her one of Europe's most sought-after, fought-over, and talked-about designers. She quotes an old proverb in her preface to *French Style*, "The best soups are made in old pots." Old pots are what she uses to contain

PREVIOUS PAGE The eye is drawn to texture rather than pattern in this simple, streamlined London living room in a house designed by architect India Mahdavi. The natural colours of the linen-covered sofas with velvet cushions and the basalt and wood fireplace give the room an earthy but still luxurious feel.

LEFT AND ABOVE The extravagant cast bronze and aluminium surround of this free-standing clock (left) in furniture designer Mark Brazier-Jones' London home is a contrast to the earthy brickwork behind it and the cowhide-covered chair (above). A green neon light glows softly from a corner of the room to add a modern twist to an interior dominated by many classic pieces of furniture.

NEXT PAGE Ornately carved furniture and gold accents combine with plain walls and floors and Mexican yucca plants to give Mark Brazier-Jones' living room a Baroque Latin feel. Plush fabrics contrast with the rawness of the logs stacked in wall cavities.

her signature ingredients. Luxurious, well chosen, and classic designs mix together to create her Timeless looks. When Putman designs, she doesn't create a place that "looks great for one year and dates in five years". She states: "I believe in classics, I believe in style."

Putman's sage-like words are the maxims behind the sensibility. Here, the best styles of the past blend with contemporary looks. From interior designer Anouska Hempel's Turkish gulet to Mark Brazier-Jones' conquistador style, old-world heirlooms and new-world chic mix together in these homes. From this, a contemporary version of Timeless emerges, shiny and new.

Timeless's forefather is undoubtedly classicism itself. Inspired by the great, glorious Roman empire, classicism has continually threaded its way through design's history, embodying symbols of wealth, sophistication, prestige, and, of course, glamour. The style defines "class" itself: glamorous homes were once measured in terms of how many columns, porticos, pedestals, and pilasters they had.

ABOVE Quills in cobalt blue pots above a sombre black fireplace are Christian Astuguevieille's own design. The inspiration was drawn from the primitive cultures that inform Astuguevieille's work. Quills are also used in many of his jewellery designs. Fabric wrapped around furniture neutralizes the shapes in this apartment, part of a grand 1870s building in Paris. The strong, modern forms and colours of the furniture sit like jewels in the pale rooms, which are decorated with Renaissance-inspired stuccowork.

RIGHT Classical stuccowork has been painted white to provide a delicate backdrop to a modern glass table and high-tech lights in Astuguevieille's apartment. The jewellery, accessories, and furniture designer combines the two extremes of old-world traditionalism and new-world modernism.

ABOVE Fashion and interior designer Anouska Hempel remodelled this 28-metre (93-foot) twin-engined Turkish gulet, creating a simple and elegant yacht with a Japanese feel. The five-sailed yacht, which cruises the Mediterranean Sea, sleeps up to eight guests and a staff of five. Up to fifty people can be aboard for cocktails and sixteen can dine in style and comfort. The traditional wooden exterior and simple, Zen-like interior conceal state-of-the-art audio/visual and communication systems.

Roman buildings still exemplify Timeless glamour. The buildings, like artworks, have lasted in all their glory. Take, for example, one of ancient Rome's greatest achievements, the Pantheon, whose poured dome was the largest in existence even until the 20th century. Another great legacy of the Romans is the bath. Of these, among the tallest and grandest are the famous baths of Caracalla, built around AD 217, occupying 140,000 square metres (1.5 million square feet). Sophisticated and stylish, these hotbeds of hedonism were an intrinsic part of Rome's glory and, as some say, its downfall.

Rome has become a Timeless byword for wealth, grandeur, and style. To prove it, the Romanesque style arises in contemporary design like a phoenix, over and over again. Donato Bramante (1441–1514), an architect inspired by the ruins of ancient Rome, ignited the

Renaissance's creative blaze. His buildings, along with the powerful religious establishment of the time, sought to recreate Rome's former glory. More than 400 years later, dictator Benito Mussolini also sought to rejuvenate Rome's great past when he reinvented neo-classicism in the 1920s and '30s. In sweeping empire style, his commissions included designing entire towns, such as Sabaudia in Italy.

Classicism threads its way through the interiors featured here. It makes the Timeless heart beat in the home of interior doyenne Jacqueline Morabito. She has reinterpreted Italian style in her own quietly elegant way, blending stripped-down Roman classicism with the modern forms of the Bauhaus. Morabito breathes life into this aesthetic with Renaissance-style reliefs, contemporary sculpture, and baroque chandeliers sitting side-by-side with streamlined furnishings.

ABOVE The dominant texture on Anouska Hempel's boat, *Beluga*, is wood – pine, ash, and teak – delicately balanced with plain black and white cushions. Black-and-white stripes on the carpets make a striking contrast with the wooden deck.

NEXT PAGE The neutral colours of natural fibres and wood create a restful environment on Anouska Hempel's boat. All clutter is hidden from view in carefully arranged straw and cane storage baskets, which blend subtly with the wooden fittings.

ABOVE Voluminous white taffeta curtains cocoon the dining room in Paul Maenz's Berlin home. Light reflected from the hard wooden floor and modern but delicate pieces of furniture – dining chairs designed in 1958 by Charles and Ray Eames and a bare, utilitarian chair designed in the early 20th century by Gerrit Rietveld – give a feeling of purity.

Classicism is reinterpreted in the Paris apartment of designer Patrice Tatard, who indulges in the Roman penchant for bathing. In his interior, a Roman-style pool is the focal point of the house. All the bedrooms, the kitchen, the office, and the gym "lead to Rome", a 10-metre (30-foot) swimming pool flanked by marble pillars. Here Patrice Tatard has gone a step further and outdone the Romans by installing overhead fans to simulate sultry breezes and create lapping waves. It's a Timeless thought: imagine what the ancient Romans could have done with the technology we have today.

Another twist on classicism is apparent in the stuccowork that creates a backdrop for the apartment of jewellery, accessory, and furniture designer Christian Astuguevieille. The 1870s Paris building pays tribute to its Timeless architectural lineage, with Astuguevieille's collection of works from primitive cultures providing a stunning

counterpoint. Textures such as velvet chair covers and feathery quills contrast with the smooth, white, classical backdrop.

Classicism fell from grace after the First World War. Angry young designers in the 1920s and '30s rebelled against the ancient world and all it stood for. By doing so, Timeless took on a new, much-needed direction. Spearheading the revolt was the Bauhaus, based in Germany and inspired by visionary Walter Gropius. The Bauhaus combined all the creative arts under one umbrella, or as Gropius said, "all artistic creativity into a unity, to reunite all artistic disciplines into a new architecture". Timeless was about to be reborn.

Combined with cubism, the early 20th-century's art movement, the style insurrection was clean lined, sleek, and, at the time, seen as very, very modern. With the outbreak of the Second World War, the movement decamped to America, continuing to inspire and influence

ABOVE A leather and rosewood-faced moulded plywood chair and footstool designed in 1956 by Charles and Ray Eames complement the enormous panels of American cherrywood in Paul Maenz's living room. The imposing horizontal strips of Plexiglass in blue, black, beige, and red on the wall are a work made especially for the room by Gerwald Rockenschaub.

NEXT PAGE Light floods into the hallway of Paul Maenz's home from a skylight set in a section of high ceiling. A mirrored mosaic wall by John Armleder and a large painting, *La Jeune Femme Etonnée*, by Julien Michel, give the room a feeling of airy spaciousness. The bicycle against the wall is an artwork by Maurizio Cattalan.

ABOVE The Miami Beach home of sculptor Michelle Oka Doner is a celebration of local flora and fauna mixed comfortably with references from opulent historical periods. A Roman revival chair from St Petersburg dated 1806 basks in the sunlight along with various tropical leaves and a collection of books. The floors were laid in white Italian marble to reflect the sunlight.

RIGHT The original 1960s gilded dressing table in Michelle Oka Doner's dressing room is topped with smooth, white Italian marble. A "Palm Cosmos" chair cast in bronze by Oka Doner has a back made from a piece of Sable palm.

NEXT PAGE A majestic Egyptian revival chair stands resplendent before Michelle Oka Doner's gleaming white living room. At night the room is lit only by candlelight from Oka Doner's cast bronze "Burning Bushes" candelabras.

ABOVE Interior designer Andrée Putman's Paris apartment has a timeless quality that characterizes her style. Much of her work is in black, grey, and white, and combines a broadly eclectic but complementary collection of objects and furniture from different periods. The sober use of colour enables her spaces to transcend fashions in decoration and stand the test of time.

architects such as Ludwig Mies van der Rohe, Frank Lloyd Wright, Adolf Loos, and Richard Neutra. Later, the borderless aesthetic became known as International Style.

Timeless veered off in another direction with the technology of the 1950s. The decade's new take on design influences gallery owner Paul Maenz's Berlin apartment. "I think it was design's most extraordinary period. It was exciting; it was inventive," he enthuses. Just as the Russian Sputnik mission in the 1950s paved the way for man's first step on the moon in 1969, so design was beginning to extend its boundaries, pioneering new styles of the future.

Timeless loves the Charles and Ray Eames lounger, an icon of the time, defining all its design aspirations. The leather and rosewood lounge chair and ottoman were made as a one-off in 1955 for the film

director Billy Wilder and have become coveted pieces. For Maenz, it's one of his most-loved possessions. "The chair followed me for 30 years everywhere I've lived," says Maenz of the chair and footstool. "It's a faithful companion to me, like a dog." A piece like this, which transcends decades and still looks modern, is quite simply immortal.

In the future, Timeless will revere Philippe Starck's work. Students will study him and lecturers will talk about his vision. Starck has become, in his lifetime, nothing short of a celebrity. You can see why with his Le Moult house in Paris. Here, as ever, his design is a stage set, putting the occupants on show. The whole interior is like a Greek amphitheatre. Everything is white and transparent, creating a canvas for the select pieces such as the poetic shape of André Dubreuil's "Spine" chair. The final effect is one of effortless elegance.

ABOVE Sheer curtains provide an unobtrusive barrier between the living area and bedroom in Andrée Putman's apartment, allowing light to flood the entire space. Light is an important feature of Putman's interiors. The décor in her apartment has a quiet elegance that features a subtle mix of colours, and interesting contrasts of luxurious and simple objects, softness and graphics.

ABOVE A wrought-iron chair designed in 1988 by André Dubreuil is an elegant decorative complement to the iron balustrade on the stairs in the living room of the Paris Le Moult house designed by Philippe Starck.

LEFT A glass desk in the Starck-designed house, supported at the back by the wall of the study and underneath by wrought iron, overlooks the living area.

NEXT PAGE An open living space surrounds a 10-metre (33-foot) pool in Patrice Tatard's Paris apartment. At each end of the pool is a fireplace built into the wall, one of which is mirrored from floor to ceiling.

From classicism to cubism, the past is the lifeblood of Timeless, but for it to continue, Timeless must keep re-creating itself. In modern design, it is interesting to look at the pieces created today that in years to come will become classics. At the moment designers and architects like Ron Arad, Nigel Coates, Tom Dixon, Marc Newson, Jasper Morrison, Matthew Hilton — the list is added to every day — are re-shaping and reinterpreting Timeless and its old friend, classicism.

Perhaps that's the illusion of Timeless. In some ways, it is everything at once: past, present, and future, and all of the homes featured here have this kind of immortal style. They speak of their time and place but yearn for transcendence. See them in twenty years and they still won't have dated. Frank Gehry would certainly approve.

ABOVE A clear, deep, plunge pool set in pale stone and flanked by plants in white pots is a relief from the intense heat and vibrant colour of the Tunisian landscape. The simplicity and colour of the arrangement offers a Zen-like sense of freshness and purity at the seaside home of architect Toni Facella Sensi.

RIGHT Tall, vaulted ceilings in the summer living area of Toni Facella Sensi's home provide a cool haven from the heat of the sun. Ornately tiled floors and candelabras contrast with refreshing whitewashed walls and pale cane chairs to give a feeling of old-fashioned colonial elegance. A series of arches leads the eye to an open courtyard and another seating area beyond.

Exotic glamour has truly international parameters –

locations might include an Indian fort,

a Thai seaside refuge, or a Moroccan palace.

Exotic places are about escape, sensual pleasures,

and being surrounded with colours, textures

and scenery that evoke an atmosphere of fantasy.

PREVIOUS PAGE An intricate cornucopia of gold stencils decorate the walls of Mary McFadden's New York home.

LEFT Arched mirrors form an altar-like centrepiece in Mary McFadden's bedroom and a silk-screened Byzantine calendar crowns the gilded ceiling. Much of the inspiration for the interior design of the apartment came from Byzantine churches.

ABOVE Fashion designer Mary McFadden's living room shimmers as light reflects on walls and ceilings covered in gold leaf and elaborate stencils. The richly decorated room mixes furniture and ornaments from around the world to evoke an atmosphere of ancient Byzantium.

Exotic places seduce us. "Romance is the glamour," as writer Amanda Cross says, "which turns the dust of everyday life into a golden haze". Like fairytales, the sights and sounds of distant cultures and far-off lands have an irresistible charm. Here, contemporary design embarks on a love affair with Exotic, weaving the sensual pleasures of far-away places into its own rich tapestry.

Exotic loves to escape. For some, like fashion designers Mary McFadden and Matthew Williamson, Exotic is a journey within the imagination, involving travel from the kitchen to the living room in Exotic surroundings. For many of us, Exotic implies a journey to distant shores. We hanker after misty mountains, tropical rainforests, and sandy deserts. We want to abandon our customary haunts. Exotic is about leaving our everyday lives behind and playing make-believe.

ABOVE A delicate tent made of hand-blocked and embroidered cotton fabric panels covers a fountain courtyard in the Umaid Bhawan Palace in Jodhpur, India. The 347-room palace was built between 1929 and 1944 by 3,000 artisans in the traditional Rajput style with an Indian-influenced art deco interior. This room serves as a restaurant in the winter months.

RIGHT Once one of the largest private residences in the w[...] Bhawan Palace is now a hotel as well as the residence [...] Gaj Singh II of Marwar. The interior of the central d[...] 33 metres [...]

ABOVE A luxurious bedroom in the Amanjena Hotel has a high domed ceiling that creates a feeling of spaciousness. The cool tiled floor subtly echoes the gold mosaic-like fabric of the daybed.

ABOVE RIGHT The delicate gold silk fabric on the daybed in a bedroom of the Amanjena Hotel is reminiscent of a shimmering mosaic wall.

LEFT The pared-down Moroccan style of the Amanjena Hotel near Marrakech in Morocco is the work of architect Ed Tuttle. This imperial and serene private living area has its own master bedroom upstairs that overlooks the central *bassin* seen overleaf.

Whether it is mental or physical, adventure is what makes Exotic's heart beat faster. Take, for example, the home of fashion designer Mary McFadden. Step in to her one-bedroom downtown Manhattan apartment and you are transported to a world of Byzantine splendour. Gold, glittering gold, is everywhere. While nothing in the apartment is actually Byzantine, the objets d'art hail from past cultures, such as a 13th-century Mexican funerary statue, a Tang altar table, and Japanese candlesticks dating from the Edo period (1605–1867).

Matthew Williamson is mentally transported whenever he steps through his door. Here, English eccentricity mixes with Exotic and the Orient meets *Saturday Night Fever*. His interiors are an extension of his clothes; his flair for colour, texture, and style graces his house as much

PREVIOUS PAGE The central *bassin* of the Amanjena Hotel was originally a holding pool used to collect irrigation water from the High Atlas Mountains. The rooms of the hotel extend from the *bassin*, connected by cool corridors of dusky pink arches and columns.

ABOVE Mirrored wooden walls bring lush vegetation into a bathroom that looks out onto a private garden at the Amanpuri Hotel on the island of Phuket in Thailand. Rooms are open to the outside as much as possible to provide cooling ventilation.

as his models. Williamson changes his interiors as often as most of us change our clothes, so his home feels like it is constantly in motion.

While mind travel has its allure, so does actually packing your bags and leaving town. There is nothing quite like a real adventure to Exotic lands. So let's take a cab to the airport and fly off to some of the world's most enchanting locations…

Travel writer Paul Theroux once said, "Travel is glamorous in retrospect." He obviously hadn't experienced Aman hotels, founded by hotelier Adrian Zecha. In Zecha's places, the beauty is in being there, and the actual moment is as glamorous as the memory.

What is striking about the Aman properties is the way they effortlessly respond to the cultures they reside in. Aside from "culture-specific design as understated as it is sophisticated", Zecha strives for "service that emphasizes the individual; a resort size that assures both a

private and a memorable guest experience". With such a mission it is no wonder the Aman has its design devotees.

Time to board our first-class flight to Thailand to the original resort first-hand, now one of twelve dotted like a string of glittering diamonds around the globe. We're in good company here; the likes of Pierce Brosnan, Naomi Campbell, and Prince Andrew are Aman regulars. We're going to play at being part of the "Amanjunkies", a set of latter-day Marie Antoinettes, who love to pretend they are castaways.

Amanpuri ("place of peace" in Sanskrit) was designed by architect Ed Tuttle. Opened in 1988 in Phuket, Thailand, the hotel is on an island connected to Phang-Na province by a bridge, so the whole Amanpuri complex is surrounded by an expanse of tranquil sea.

The hotel was built amid a coconut plantation connected by elevated walkways. Adjacent to the resort are 30 Amanpuri villas, where

ABOVE The Amanpuri Hotel in Thailand, designed by architect Ed Tuttle, is based on the designs of Sri Lankan architect Geoffrey Bawa, who mixed indigenous traditions with a vision of modernity. This Zen-like bedroom decorated with Thai art and antiques, fresh white linen, and native wood has an outdoor *sala* or traditional Thai open-sided pavilion.

"A glamorous place is as much about creating a sanctuary for the guest to feel completely at peace" says Dale Keller, an architect who also worked on the Amanpuri's design. A pavilion with a traditional Thai pitched roof provides an elegant shelter from the hot tropical sun at the Amanpuri Hotel, where guests can enjoy the view over the Andaman Sea and be waited on by attentive staff.

There is a strong sense of theatre in the shrine-like compound of the Amanpuri Hotel, one of the top half-dozen resorts in the world. Built in 1988, the resort is set on the west coast of the island of Phuket in 40 hectares (100 acres) of coconut plantations. The serene black-slate pool provides an impressive centrepiece to the resort. Guests sleep in pavilions that are connected by elevated walkways supported by stilts.

ABOVE One of thirteen luxury tents at the Rajvilas Hotel in Jaipur, Rajasthan evokes the colonial ambience of the Raj and transports the guest to a time of glamour and adventure. An elaborately embroidered canopy floats above the air-conditioned room.

RIGHT A sunken Italian marble bath strewn with vibrant flowers – in which one bathes in the exotic landscape outside – overlooks a private walled garden at the Rajvilas Hotel.

NEXT PAGE A 250-year-old Hindu temple is the centrepiece of a lotus-filled pond at the Rajvilas Hotel. Once a *haveli* or mansion belonging to Maharaja Jai Singh II, the property is now a luxury hotel set in 12 hectares (30 acres) of formal gardens.

the architecture is a mix of the traditional and modern. Service is the fifth star here, there are five mind-reading staff for each guest, and, as guests leave, the staff tie orchids around their suitcase handles. Mies van der Rohe was right: God really is in the details here.

Time to jet off to our next fix, Marrakech. Once one of the most important artistic and cultural centres in the Islamic world, Marrakech is where Africa meets Islam, and where both meet the West: travellers have stamped a well-worn path through here since the 1960s. Away from the food stalls, the hustlers, the snake charmers, and the street acrobats is another Aman haunt – the Amanjena.

Again, Ed Tuttle has combined local architecture with contemporary Western tastes to create a type of Moroccan palace. It is almost imperial in scale, and makes the most of the surrounding space,

ABOVE James Goldstein's house is cantilevered on the edge of a cliff overlooking the Benedictine Canyon in Beverly Hills and has views from every room. Below the house is a forest of palm trees and tropical foliage. Architect John Lautner built the house in 1963 for the Sheats family and remodelled it for its present owner, James Goldstein, who bought it in 1972.

LEFT Dynamic triangular roof lines in the Goldstein house are punctuated by hundreds of small skylights made from inverted drinking glasses impaled in the roof. Lautner is known for his bold geometry and exciting use of materials.

NEXT PAGE Massive glass windows dissolve the visual barrier between building and nature and provide an uninterrupted view of the carpet of twinkling lights below. The glass walls retract electronically to create a spectacular deck that ends in an acute angle.

light, and water, in its design. Amanjena's forty pavilions and six two-storey *maisons* fan out from the central *bassin* in concentric circles, separated by reflection pools. In the evenings, lanterns and candles cast dappled shadows around the vast pools.

And the rooms! Imagine this: we're now in one of its pavilions, with a high, domed ceiling, a king-size bed, a daybed, and an open fireplace for the winters. The bathroom, set among a lush garden, has a tub made of green Moroccan marble. Each *maison* has its own pool, garden, outdoor fireplace, and a dedicated butler.

Our next destination is Jodhpur, Rajasthan, India. In a place of unrelenting sun, where camels tread over the soft sands of the Thar Desert, is the striking former home of Maharaja Umaid Bhawan in Jodhpur. Completed in 1944, it is the last great palace to have been

ABOVE Smooth polished teak in the dressing room of Lekha and Ranjan Poddar's house near Delhi in India, contrasts with the raw concrete blocks surrounding the doorway. Architect Inni Chatterjee and interior designer Samiir Wheaton designed the striking modernist house.

LEFT The flowing contours of a long dining table designed by Samiir Wheaton in Burma teak imitates the drape of a textile. The red lacquer trays are Burmese.

NEXT PAGE Hariett Selling Canepa's Los Angeles home was designed by John Lautner for Mr and Mrs Alden Schwimmer in 1982. Douglas fir timber and roughly cut stone are used with simplicity in a design with Japanese references.

ABOVE The dressing room in Patrice and Magali Nourissat's Paris home is a cornucopia of separate drawers and shelves that provide a tailored home for garments and every type of accessory. Two 19th-century busts and the grey accents in the woodwork are highlighted by smooth grey carpet. The glossy lemon-coloured wood is highly varnished fir. The rooms are the work of Patrice, an interior designer, and are influenced by many different historical themes.

RIGHT A monumental stone bas-relief of a hunting scene, inspired by the opulent tapestries of Normandy, dominates the bedroom. A rich colour scheme of cobalt blue and mandarin orange in the ensuite bathroom areas complements the neutral colours of the bedroom.

built in India. The result is a mix of traditional Indian styles and art deco that pays homage to the fairytale past of Rajasthan.

While in India, we can peer inside the home of the Poddar family. Here, Exotic's roles have been reversed and the East has welcomed the West. Architect Inni Chatterjee and designer Samiir Wheaton have blown away the traditions of India and replaced them with minimalist styling. Western modernity's hard edges are allayed by the East's curvy lines and colour accents.

Time to come back to our own homes. Having been away, we realize how important Exotic is to us. We need Exotic to spice up our interiors and our lives. However it is defined, Exotic, with its power and mystique, turns everyday life into a golden, glowing haze. And, by doing so, Exotic expands our horizons and opens our minds.

PREVIOUS PAGE Fashion designer Matthew Williamson's flamboyant use of colour is as evident in his London home as it is in his fashion collections. He has a particular passion for pink, found in many shades throughout the house. The living room is one of the more sober rooms in the house, mixing modern items with English and Oriental pieces.

ABOVE The chinoiserie wallpaper in the hall of Matthew Williamson's house was copied and enlarged from a Victorian print that Matthew found at the Victoria and Albert Museum in London. Luminous flecks of colour have been added to the hand-painted design.

RIGHT Colourful textiles, a glittering chandelier, and an Indian mural on the bathroom wall visible from the bedroom give this space an exotic Eastern twist. Pink – the colour that 1960s Vogue Editor Diana Vreeland proclaimed "the navy blue of India" – adorns the walls and table.

SEDATE

Sedate glamour has its own kind of riches.

Its treasures are often simple luxuries,

like an abundance of space and light.

Its colours are never brash or showy.

Sedate is quietly thoughtful and contemplative;

its tempo is measured.

PREVIOUS PAGE An arched roof of glass bricks lets maximum light into the bedroom of Pierre Lombard's home in Johannesburg, creating a feeling of space.

ABOVE The bathroom in Pierre Lombard's house is a stage for indulging the senses. The free-standing bath is carefully positioned to take in the spectacular vista and the room is perfect for complete repose.

LEFT The bedroom on the preceding page is on a mezzanine above the pool and deck seen here. Architect Pierre Lombard has made full use of the magnificent views and strong South African sunlight.

As the ancient Aboriginal proverb goes, "the more you know the less you need". Sedate believes this with all its soul. It has no time for Glamour's flashy pretensions. Whenever Glamour parties itself into oblivion, Glamour goes to Sedate's recovery clinic.

This sensibility has often arrived throughout history as a tonic after periods of chaos and carnage, toil and turmoil. Sedate sweeps in to wipe the slate clean, to bring everything back to basics.

Sedate is perceived as such by our five senses. Smooth surfaces soothe frayed nerves. Homes that smell good take us back to our childhood and a well-stocked kitchen reminds us that we will never go hungry. Colour provides Sedate's visually gentle backdrop. Sedate follows Andrée Putman's advice not to "use colours that exist too much. Life always comes with its own colours: your friends, flowers, things. So you don't have to have so much of it in your décor."

And then, of course, there's Sedate's sixth sense – spirit.

Sedate combines spirit and home. For fêted Mexican architect Luis Barragan, the two are inextricably linked. And they go way back, hand in hand, like old friends. "It is impossible to understand art and the glory of its history without avowing religious spirituality and the mythical roots that lead us to the very being of the artistic phenomenon," he said. "Without the one or the other, there would be no Egyptian pyramids, nor those of ancient Mexico."

To discover its spiritual past, Sedate has cast its net far and wide, towards East and West. It has searched the ascetic quarters of the contemplative orders and emulated the economy and craftsmanship of the Shakers. It has travelled to Japan, sat on its haunches, and studied Zen. As Heinrich Engel wrote, "A room in a Western home is human

ABOVE The Sculptured House was conceived in the 1950s by architect Charles Deaton. The house famously appeared in Woody Allen's film *Sleeper* as a backdrop to life in the year 2173.

RIGHT Deaton ran out of money, and when philanthropist and investor John Huggins bought the almost derelict architectural icon in 1999, it was home to a den of wolves. One of the challenges of restoring it involved building everything in curves. Everything had to be custom-made, right down to the banisters.

NEXT PAGE The house swirls atop Genesee Mountain, where views from the windows take in Denver and the Continental Divide. Furniture in the sunken living room include an "Egg" chair and four vintage "Swan" chairs.

ABOVE The office, tucked away in its own quiet, curvaceous corner, looks out onto the terrace and to the mountains beyond. It is the perfect place to think: the table was designed by Deaton, the chair by Arne Jacobsen, and the office chair by d'Alberto Meda. In the evenings, light from downlighters sited in the circular ceiling above delineates the space.

LEFT When lit, the cone-shaped fireplace burns a ring of flame and brings warmth into the living room. As Deaton left the plan uncompleted, Huggins employed his daughter Charlee and her architect husband, Nicholas Antonopoulos, to fill in the blanks. Together they devised the fixtures and furnishings the house never had, like this fireplace, which somehow fits in seamlessly with Deaton's 1950s style.

ABOVE With his truly wonderful eye for colour, Mexican architect Luis Barragan proved modernism need not be clinical or monochrome. The colours he used were often derived from natural pigments rather than the chemical-based paints that many modernists tended to use. In the Gilardi House in Mexico City, the sun's rays stream down on lavender walls from a skylight above.

without man's presence, for man's memory lingers in the multiple devices of decoration, furniture and utility. A room in a Japanese residence becomes human only through man's presence. Thus an empty room provides the very space where man's spirit can move freely and where his thoughts can reach the very limits of potential."

Sedate follows other spiritual notions, such as the idea that cleanliness is next to godliness (and we're not just talking hygiene). Cleanliness is about order, something, oddly, we often forget about in urban life. To have an inner equilibrium, Sedate needs everything to be in its place. Interior designer Kelly Hoppen puts order at the top of her priorities. "I like coming home to find everything is just so. I like order and harmony but also comfort. Homes should be a retreat."

So just when did Sedate make its entrance over the last century? It has appeared like a white knight and swept off its glamorous damsel

in distress. Sedate first galloped into interiors after the Great War. Horrified by the events of the war, it turned to Mies van der Rohe's catchphase, "less is more". Design shed its chintz and glitz, and stripped homes and furnishings down to their bare bones. Everything superfluous was banished for clean, refined lines.

To go with the pared-back forms, Sedate demanded a new colour. Interior decorator (and wife of writer Somerset Maugham) Syrie Maugham introduced the spectrum's most pure hue: white. Her enormous drawing room, on the King's Road in London, featured sofas slip-covered in white satin, a white geometric carpet, white wooden tables, white velvet lampshades, and flowers in various shades of white: oyster white, plaster white, and eggshell white. At the time, it caused a sensation. Overnight, it became a classic look, transported to Hollywood in a snowstorm of white frothy floor rugs and draperies.

ABOVE Barragan thought himself a landscape architect rather than a designer. As he wrote in *Contemporary Architects*: "I believe that architects should design gardens to be used, as much as the houses they build, to develop a sense of beauty and the taste and inclination towards the fine arts and other spiritual values." Here, nature and architecture reside together as natural soulmates.

"At the time, white in all shades was frequently used almost to the exclusion of other colours in certain fashion houses. In the intervening three decades, with the rapid and almost frenzied pre-war and post-war succession of fads, gimmicks, trends, and trick schemes, white was almost forgotten," comments the designer Michael Taylor, himself a fan of Maugham, in his autobiographical essay, "*A New Look at Decorating*".

After the Second World War, Sedate was summoned on its steed. Architect Charles Deaton remembered the influence of white decades later in the 1960s. His post-war opus, the Sculptured House, all curves and rounded lines, was snow-white, inside and out.

Deaton's house blends in seamlessly with the snowy mountain landscape. Unlike the clean-cut lines of the modernists, his home's

ABOVE LEFT Fashion designer Thierry Mugler maximizes light and space in his apartment in Paris. While Mugler is renowned for his eclectic clothing designs, his apartment is serene and sedate. Light pours in through slatted blinds in a play of light and shadow.

ABOVE The ground floor of this three-floored penthouse is a series of three rooms joined together. The dining area is bathed in light from large adjacent windows.

RIGHT A large mirror on the wall behind the dining table echoes the geometric shapes of the room, making it seem spacious. The whole setting feels like a still life, where the flowers are the focal point.

ABOVE One wall of the bathroom in this Berlin appartment, designed by architect
Stefan Sterf, is transparent so that the light from this room is the main light source
for the bedroom on the other side of the wall. The shiny citrus-coloured floor gives a
polish to the fresh minimal interior.

LEFT Doors from the large, open-plan living area of Christian and Carolin
Heldmann's Berlin apartment lead to tiny, intimate rooms. Stairs covered in
artificial grass go up to a "bridge" that leads to bedrooms, a small office
area, and balcony.

lines were all fluid and free flowing. He followed his own laws, inspired by the organic forms of nature. "I believe people look better and feel better among curves, that curvilinear designs make people feel less confined," Deaton once said. "Curved buildings provide a natural setting for curved people."

While white makes the perfect interior, it also makes the ideal exterior. As author Lewis Mumford says, "White and white alone fully reflects the surrounding lights; white and white alone gives a pure blue or lavender shadow against the sunlight. In short, except on a grey day, white is anything but white." Deaton's building, perched atop Genesee Mountain in Colorado, reflects nature's dramatic light show.

ABOVE Reflective surfaces increase the feeling of space in Voon Wong's apartment. The interplay of light and subtle colours gives the apartment an air of sophisticated glamour.

RIGHT In the living room of Voon Wong's London apartment everything is designed to maximize light and space. A white sofa from B&B Italia contrasts with hanging lights from Vistosi.

NEXT PAGE The living room of London-based interior designer Kelly Hoppen has been created from two rooms to create one large space, where fireplaces stand back-to-back in a broad central column.

ABOVE Tall windows are shielded by light curtains in Hoppen's bedroom. The earthy colour scheme of cream, khaki, taupe, and chocolate brown is relaxing and comforting, making the room the perfect place to slumber.

LEFT Even the bathroom echoes Hoppen's philosophy that the home should be a retreat. Here, the bather can recline beside spring flowers in the old-fashioned grandeur of a roll-top bath. With centered taps, the tub is perfect for bathing *à deux*.

After the stockmarket crash of the 1980s, Sedate once again came to rescue homes from their designer excesses. A whitewash was again needed to wipe the interior design slate clean of its wanton reds, bossy blacks, and glutinous gold leaf. There was a need for order and cleanliness, and this time, Sedate went all the way.

Sedate returned, but this time in the guise of cool white modernism, stripped of its highbrow morals. The house was no longer, as Le Corbusier envisaged, a "machine for living in", instead it became a retreat from the world, a place of quiet refuge. Sedate was "the new

simplicity" and set the scene for minimalism, a look where nothing but the bare essentials exist.

British architect John Pawson, who trained in Japan for many years, and his former partner, the Italian-born architect Claudio Silverstrin were Sedate's new avant garde in the early 1990s. At the heart of their philosophy was the aim to clear out the distraction and mess of modern Western life and give the home a Zen-like spirit of purity and repose. Silverstrin's home is like the Cistercian monasteries he admires. The monks believed architecture was a form of prayer. For Silverstrin, the home is a place of contemplation and solace. Here, glamour does not come from the addition of colour, fabrics, furniture, or any other household items. Silverstrin's spaces are often used as spiritual retreats as well as dwellings. His architecture draws off natural elements, such as proportion, light, and space. In many ways

ABOVE Terence Conran once said, "It seems incongruous that the bedroom, which is by far the most personal room in the house, is also the most neglected." Here, the bedroom in Carolyn and Christian Hall's home is a perfect mixture of texture and colour, warmth and light.

RIGHT Light falls through a curtained window onto an elliptical tub in Carolyn and Christian Hall's home in Newcastle, England. Bathrooms, one of the only completely private rooms in the home, have become true retreats. This one, with candles by the bathtub, is an inviting place to luxuriate. A large, sculptural heater nearby provides warmth and comfort.

ABOVE The interior of the Devi Garh Hotel, in these pictures taken for *Elle Deco*, is a modern, minimalist take on traditional Rajput design. Cool white marble mined from local quarries is used extensively throughout the palace, broken by flashes of gold, silver and semi-precious stones like malachite and lapis lazuli. Traditional materials and motifs are used in the contemporary designs to create an environment that blends consummate luxury with utter simplicity.

the glamour comes from complete simplicity. As his former colleague John Pawson says, "Phenomenology in architecture requires deliberate attention to how things are made. As Mies [van der Rohe] supposedly said 'God is in the details'. This influential school of thought not only recognizes and celebrates the basic elements of architecture (wall, floor, ceiling, etc, as horizon or boundary) but has led to a renewed interest in the sensuous qualities of materials, light, and colour, and in the symbolic, tactile significance of the joint." Like that of Cistercian monks, the only furniture is built into the walls of the rooms, becoming part of the construction itself. By paring back the interiors, the beauty comes from the building's essential structure.

The minimalists took up the Shaker creed expressed centuries earlier: "Don't make anything unless it is both necessary and useful, but

if it is both necessary and useful, don't hesitate to make it beautiful." The minimalists believe everything reaches a state of perfection where it is necessary, useful, and beautiful. For Pawson, a Georgian three-pronged fork is the perfect incarnation of a fork. Nothing can improve on it. The pieces left in these minimalist homes are pure and flawless.

A return to Sedate was welcomed with a sigh of relief by stressed-out urbanites. With many facing longer working hours, people wanted to come home to their own sanctuaries. Fashion designer Thierry Mugler and architect Voon Wong embraced the new aesthetic. The style makes the most of light and space, always a premium in the city.

For Mugler, his apartment is an oasis away from his eclectic catwalk designs. In his Paris apartment, he has used translucent accessories and reflective surfaces to maximize space. Fashion designer

ABOVE Like any traditional Indian dwelling, life revolves around courtyards at the Devi Garh Hotel. The palace has five courtyards and twenty-three large suites where there were once 250 different rooms. The spaciousness and minimal design creates a peaceful, calm environment, a respite from heat and dust of the Rajasthani plains. Lekha Poddar, whose home is seen on pages 96–97, owns the hotel.

Didier Bohbot, also in Paris, has opted for clean, cool designs with splashes of colour. In London, Voon Wong has kept his space airy by elevating part of the kitchen hob, and allowing light from side windows to reach the living area by reflecting off the glossy floor.

Sedate is glamour's reserved, serious side. It continues to bring the qualities modern life craves: silence, intimacy, inspiration, beauty, spirituality, and serenity. "Any work of architecture which does not express serenity is a mistake," said the deeply spiritual Barragan, and he's right. Sedate is a design essential; it is Glamour with soul.

As Le Corbusier once said, "Space and light and order: these are the things men need just as much as they need bread or a place to sleep." Never mind all that glitters. Sedate glamour is wise. It knows more, so it needs so much less.

ABOVE This house in the south of France, designed by Claudio Silvestrin, is inspired by medieval Cistercian monasteries. Like the monasteries, all of the furniture is built into the walls of the room. The beauty of the home does not come from the addition of colour or fabrics, but from the structure of the building itself.

RIGHT The bathroom in the Silvestrin-designed house contains just a shower and this great 2-metre (7-foot) oval bath, also designed by Claudio Silvestrin, which is carved out of a single piece of limestone.

NEXT PAGE An experiment by architect Souhed Ennemlaghi, all surfaces in Didier Bohbot's Paris apartment are covered in epoxy, giving it the cool, smooth texture of a porcelain cup.

ABOVE Much of the furniture in the Palais Bulles (Bubble Palace) was designed by fashion designer Pierre Cardin and, like all parts of the house, has rounded corners. Building of the house started in 1976 and was completed in the 1980s. Even now it is very futuristic in feel.

LEFT A circular bed with pebble-shaped pillows is in one of eight bedrooms in the house designed by architect Antti Lovag for Pierre Cardin. The oval and circular-shaped rooms create a cave-like atmosphere.

PREVIOUS PAGE A circular bath under a large round window looks out over tropical palms to the Mediterranean Sea.

NEXT PAGE All furniture and structures in the Palais Bulles, including doorways, ceilings, and fixtures, are curved, creating an extravaganza of organic shapes.

clectic allows its own personal vision to rule. These homes, out of all the glamorous places featured here, truly mirror the loves and lives of their owners. Everything within them has been chosen with great passion. These spaces become more than just homes: they become an annex and a reflection of the owner's personality. As Akiko Busch writes in *Geography of Home*, "The more we personalize our possessions, the more we are able to see ourselves in the things we own. And once we've invested ourselves in the things we own, it is difficult to be rid of them."

Take French writer, artist, and nomad, Jean Cocteau. Cocteau rarely stayed in one place, but when he did it became his physical diary, overflowing with the things he had collected: *objets d'art*, mementoes, and souvenirs. Cocteau's homes were a living record of his life and they became a kind of "show and tell" of his passions, like his final home in an 18th-century stone house in Milly-la-Forêt near Fontainebleau, complete with leopard-print spiral staircase and

ECLECTIC

Eclectic is completely liberated.

When others fret about what goes with what,

Eclectic doesn't care. It's a wild child, loose and

uninhibited. Eclectic believes rules are made

to be broken. Where Sedate extols "less is more",

Eclectic cries "less is a bore".

ABOVE Fashion designer Didier Bohbot wanted to create a complete sanctuary away from the colour and texture that his work involves. The furniture is built to resemble sculptures inside the space – all light switches, handles, and appliances are hidden behind panels. Even the taps on the bath are only revealed when a panel is pushed.

RIGHT The mammoth dining table (also seen on the previous page) is 6 metres (20 feet) long and hides all of the kitchen appliances at one end. Bohbot didn't want the appartment to be too cold, so to inject warmth and vitality, he chose vibrant accents of red and introduced flowers. The pool of water in the table serves many purposes – champagne, oysters, and caviar can cool in it, the water is sometimes coloured, or flowers can float idly.

Didier Bohbot, also in Paris, has opted for clean, cool designs with splashes of colour. In London, Voon Wong has kept his space airy by elevating part of the kitchen hob, and allowing light from side windows to reach the living area by reflecting off the glossy floor.

Sedate is glamour's reserved, serious side. It continues to bring the qualities modern life craves: silence, intimacy, inspiration, beauty, spirituality, and serenity. "Any work of architecture which does not express serenity is a mistake," said the deeply spiritual Barragan, and he's right. Sedate is a design essential; it is Glamour with soul.

As Le Corbusier once said, "Space and light and order: these are the things men need just as much as they need bread or a place to sleep." Never mind all that glitters. Sedate glamour is wise. It knows more, so it needs so much less.

ABOVE This house in the south of France, designed by Claudio Silvestrin, is inspired by medieval Cistercian monasteries. Like the monasteries, all of the furniture is built into the walls of the room. The beauty of the home does not come from the addition of colour or fabrics, but from the structure of the building itself.

RIGHT The bathroom in the Silvestrin-designed house contains just a shower and this great 2-metre (7-foot) oval bath, also designed by Claudio Silvestrin, which is carved out of a single piece of limestone.

NEXT PAGE An experiment by architect Souhed Ennemlaghi, all surfaces in Didier Bohbot's Paris apartment are covered in epoxy, giving it the cool, smooth texture of a porcelain cup.

if it is both necessary and useful, don't hesitate to make it beautiful." The minimalists believe everything reaches a state of perfection where it is necessary, useful, and beautiful. For Pawson, a Georgian three-pronged fork is the perfect incarnation of a fork. Nothing can improve on it. The pieces left in these minimalist homes are pure and flawless.

A return to Sedate was welcomed with a sigh of relief by stressed-out urbanites. With many facing longer working hours, people wanted to come home to their own sanctuaries. Fashion designer Thierry Mugler and architect Voon Wong embraced the new aesthetic. The style makes the most of light and space, always a premium in the city.

For Mugler, his apartment is an oasis away from his eclectic catwalk designs. In his Paris apartment, he has used translucent accessories and reflective surfaces to maximize space. Fashion designer

ABOVE Like any traditional Indian dwelling, life revolves around courtyards at the Devi Garh Hotel. The palace has five courtyards and twenty-three large suites where there were once 250 different rooms. The spaciousness and minimal design creates a peaceful, calm environment, a respite from heat and dust of the Rajasthani plains. Lekha Poddar, whose home is seen on pages 96–97, owns the hotel.

PREVIOUS PAGE Palais Bulles, on Cap d'Antibes in the south of France, is made up of a labyrinth of 28 concrete spheres that spill down the hillside.

ABOVE The Long Bar in the Philippe Starck-designed Sanderson Hotel is a 28-metre (80-foot) long onyx rectangle that glows from within, topped by matt stainless steel. The surreal bar stools have silver-leaf frames and upholstered backs printed with a photograph of a woman's eye. The hotel's design is a glamorous combination of irony and elegance.

two gilded palm trees. As Cocteau put it, "the essential tact in daring is to know how far one can go". The only limits of his home were his own intellectual boundaries.

One of the founding fathers of Eclectic is the English king, George IV, crowned in 1821. Rebelling against his strict upbringing, George IV was a slave to his passions: philandering, drinking, gambling, and socializing. He was the playboy of his day, and his summer home, the Royal Pavilion in Brighton, was the talk of the town (and not much of it was complimentary). German architect Hermann Muthesius was to observe much later that, "it is alien to the nature of an Englishman of standing to envelop himself in luxury". So it was with a rebel yell that George IV cried, "more, more, more!"

His lavish pavilion now acts as a Mecca for those wanting divine, eclectic inspiration. His south-coast getaway combines Chinese-style decorations with magnificent furniture and furnishings. Adorned with gilded dragons, carved palm trees, and imitation bamboo staircases, the palace's style mixes Eastern exoticism with English eccentricity. Perhaps the most beautiful room of all is the music room, with a lotus-shaped chandelier and hand-painted gold-leaf scalloped roof.

Like King George IV, Eclectic loves excess. Three extravagant people stand out among some of the last century's most decadent periods in the 1920s, '30s and '60s. The most outstanding free-thinker of the 1920s was designer Eileen Gray, First Lady of the glamorous and functional. Gray, the daughter of wealthy Irish parents, broke away

ABOVE A luxurious, silver-leafed 19th-century sleigh bed in London's Sanderson Hotel is the extravagant centrepiece to a light, ethereal bedroom carpeted with a rug inspired by a letter written by Voltaire. There are no walls in the bedrooms; instead partitions between the bathroom and dressing areas are created with electronically controlled sheer white and opaque pink curtains.

NEXT PAGE An original Studio 65 "Marilyn" lips sofa from 1972 is set against flowing sheer white curtains in the lobby of the Sanderson Hotel.

ABOVE A large-scale, ethereal work by fine-art photographer Mira Bernabeu rests against a wall in Jibby Beane's bedroom. The mirror and reflective surface of the floor make the light, white space appear more spacious.

from her bourgeois background and fled to Paris. She was an odd mix of shy and uncompromising and combined and contrasted the modern, the sensual, and the exotic in her eclectic designs.

Her own home was admired by Le Corbusier, who later made use of her beautiful furniture and rugs, which have become sought-after collectors' items. While her interiors retained the charm of the *maison minimum*, she mixed zebra skins with white leather chairs, and Chinese paintings with translucent glass panels illuminated from below. Animal skins complemented Gray's voluptuous chairs, now classics. She lived, breathed, and sold glamour – her designs were so expensive they could only be bought by wealthy patrons.

The second Eclectic torch-bearer is a little-known Italian poet of the 1930s. Gabriele D'Annunzio has left to prosperity an odd mix of

eccentric beauty and ego-centric kitsch. He made his home, the Vittoriale, on the shores of Lake Garda in Italy, his own personal monument complete with mausoleum in three white stone tiers, rather like an enormous wedding cake. His aim was to tear down the sensibilities of the old bourgeois Italian villa and create something new and shocking. For example, he was rumoured to siesta in a coffin in his spare bedroom, and in his bathroom there are more than 2,000 pieces of pure junk, yet – remarkably – there's still space for a tub. He even parked a battleship – the *Puglia* – in the garden, which surges through a copse of cypress trees. Jean Cocteau believed he was "haunted by bric-a-brac", and in D'Annunzio's villa, his memory still lives on in its walls.

Danish designer Verner Panton is Eclectic's 1960s champion. He blew most perceptions of design clear out of the water. "The main

ABOVE .Jibby Beane's London gallery-cum-home is a simple, elegant space where she shows the works of the artists she represents in the same area in which she lives. Long banquettes laden with vinyl cushions contain storage space so that a look of minimalism can be maintained.

NEXT PAGE Jibby Beane's glamorous bedroom is reminiscent of the original white-on-white room designed in the 1930s by London society decorator Syrie Maugham. The look was emulated in many Hollywood movies of the period. An aluminium mannequin stands behind a white vinyl-covered "Slipper" chaise longue, both designed by Nigel Coates.

ABOVE David and Claudia Dorell's London home, designed by architects McDowell and Benedetti, is graphic in its use of bold colour and strong shapes. The work on the floor by artist Richard Woods sets the tone for a flamboyant visual statement by owners who are unafraid to express themselves. The rounded chair and footstool – designed to resemble a mother and child – is a re-issue of an "Up 5" chair created by Gaetano Pesce in 1969.

purpose of my work," he wrote, "is to provoke people into using their imaginations. Most people spend their lives in dreary grey-beige conformity, mortally afraid of using colour. By experimenting with lighting, colours, textiles, and furniture, and utilizing the latest technologies, I try to show new ways to encourage people to use their fantasy and make their surroundings more exciting." With his lurid colour schemes, funky furniture, and iconic interiors, Panton celebrated eclectic and made it popular.

Without the 1960s, design would still be a dullard. Architect Antti Lovag wove the 1960s sexual revolution into his architecture. Using sexual innuendo, his giant Palais Bulles (Bubble Palace) on the Côte d'Azur, bought by fashion maestro Pierre Cardin, is sensual and

very, very sexy. For Cardin, it may be just one of his 50 homes, but this one is a true original. When he awakes here Cardin knows exactly where he is just by looking up at the curved ceilings. Everything is curvy and womb-like, and guests walk from floor to floor down organic, winding tunnels.

Without these radicals, Eclectic would languish in the doldrums. American Jeff Sayre is another modern-day revolutionary. Like Panton, his style is suspended in time and place. Sayre injected his own fantasy into the 700-year-old Chateau Mespoulet in France. Left derelict for more than two centuries, it was restored by Sayre following architect Stewart Brand's theory that, "Every house is a work in progress. It begins with the imagination of the people who build it and is gradually

ABOVE Subtle details are combined with large controlled areas of colour in the Dorell home. A striking bed designed by Tom Climent with velvet-covered head and tailboards appears almost borderless as its finely carved white edges blend subtly with the white walls and floor. The bear-shaped chair is a piece of Victoriana made in the late 1800s.

NEXT PAGE A bank of shocking pink lacquered cupboards is the luscious focal point of the Dorell kitchen. The monolithic counter is an aggregate of pebbles and cement bound together and cast. The "Lem" stools are by the Azumis.

Pierre Staudenmeyers' Paris apartment is in a 19th-century Haussmann-style building with delicate stuccowork on the ceilings, but there the historical references end. Staudenmeyers has a passion for design from the 20th century and particularly likes objects that express themselves strongly. A brightly coloured mobile ceiling lamp by Gino Sarfatti hangs above a wall lamp by Pierre Warishe and a chest of drawers by Anne Liberati.

ABOVE An eclectic collection of modern furniture creates a subtle palette of pale colours against the detailed stuccowork and pale parquet floor in Staudenmeyers' dining room. The lamps standing on the floor are by Gino Sarfatti.

NEXT PAGE The New York home of designer Karim Rashid is filled to the rafters with his designs and art. A prolific designer of furniture, furnishings, and products, he is committed to all things contemporary and his designs seen here – what he calls "sensual minimalism" – reflect the lack of historical reference.

ABOVE Cliff and Mandy Einstein have created a gallery connected to their Los Angeles home where art is displayed for full effect in a minimalist environment – white walls, oak floors stained black, and contemporary furniture in black or white chosen for style and simplicity. The "Cesca" chairs designed by Marcel Breuer in 1928 face Ed Ruscha's *The Long Wait* (1995).

transformed, for better or for worse, by the people who occupy it down through the years."

For better, Sayre drained away the chateau's colours and instead left a playful, tactile atmosphere. Neutral tones blend the furnishings together: the sheep's skulls, sofas covered in Irish linen, and bleached wood chairs. It's a mix of everything he loves. There is even a boat, an Irish dinghy, beached in the garden. Like the building itself, Sayre has filled the chateau with memories: stern-faced Victorian dolls, wedding photos from local flea markets, and wooden busts from West Africa sit side-by-side with old basketwork and a woven rope chair.

Like Sayre, Cliff and Mandy Einstein's West Los Angeles home lives by the maxim, "Art is what you make it." Eclectic to the Einsteins is held together by a common thread: artistry and originality. The

Einstein's home is like a tribute to Eclectic's "who's who" list. Everything in this house is made by original thinkers for original thinkers. Chairs, tables, and lamps by maestros such as Le Corbusier, Marcel Breuer, Mies van der Rohe, Vico Magistretti, Eileen Gray, Isamu Noguchi, and Tobia Scarpa sit like sculptures among the paintings.

One thing that is common to all Eclectic homes is a sense of humour. Yes, fun. Betty and Felix Wasser's home in Los Angeles' Hidden Hills district near Calabasas has furniture that looks like it has come to party, while at Ian Schraeger's hotel, The Sanderson, designed by Philippe Starck, the pieces laugh at the guests. Just when you thought no one was looking one-eyed barstools keep watch and Marilyn Monroe's lips pout in the lobby. Even Eileen Gray was famed in her time for putting up a sign up on her front door, "Defense de

ABOVE This monumental sculpture, *Einstein's Place and Mark Thompson's Airplane Parts* by Nancy Rubin, 1997, is one of several outdoor pieces in the Einsteins' sculpture garden. The 9-metre (27-foot) construction is made of metal airplane parts. The Einsteins say that they have no discipline in choosing pieces, but that large-scale, dramatic pieces seem to catch their eye.

Rire" (No Laughing), to poke fun at the modernists, who she thought had no sense of humour. Eclectic, you see, has a twinkle in its eye.

All these interiors singlemindedly spell out their own taste. They are proud of who they are and what they like. Worrying about what goes with what is the last thing on Eclectic's mind. As the architect Robert Venturi wrote, "I'm for messy vitality over obvious unity... the difficult unity of inclusion rather than the easy unity of exclusion."

What we must do first is decide what we love. If you trust your taste, you celebrate Eclectic. Even taste-shaper Andrée Putman says she has "no recipe for how to combine things. But you must be sincere. And, if you are, strangely, it will succeed." Eclectic believes in itself. In many ways, it is what we should all strive for, to let our hair down and become footloose and fancy free.

ABOVE Designer Jeff Sayre has restored a French chateau that dates from the 12th century, whitewashing the walls and filling the house with pale-coloured furniture, fabrics, and natural-coloured stone, bone, and wooden objects.

RIGHT Smooth grey stones and a huge animal skull become beautiful sculptural objects on rough-hewn, Brancusi-like pedestals. Sayre's style is united by the lack of colour. Natural colours predominate: the oak floors have been bleached, fabrics and carpets are pale, and photographs are black and white.

NEXT PAGE The courtyard has been transformed into a stylized maritime garden. An Irish dinghy lies in the centre of a carefully raked expanse of gravel.

nal figure by Fornasetti is given a modern home. His work *Eve* –

g on gold ceramic plates – hangs in Betty and Felix Wasser's Los

. The sculptural, purple velvet-covered chair was designed by

gio Savarese for Dialogica.

RIGHT Betty Wasser, who has a background in modern art, designe

the help of engineers. Common materials are made glamorous h

steel tub designed by Simon Maltby reflects in the poured concrete f

white damask and grey ultrasuede chair with aluminium tubular le

DIRECTORY

HOTELS

Allegro Hotel
171 West Randolph
Chicago, Illinois 60601
USA
Tel: +1 312 236 0123
Fax: +1 312 236 3440
www.allegrochicago.com
(Boutique-hotel with modernist luxury)

Amanjena
Route de Ouarzazate, km 12
Marrakech
Morocco
Tel: +212 44 403 353
Fax: +212 44 403 477
www.amanresorts.com
(See pages 80–83)

Amanpuri
Pansea Beach, Phuket Island
Thailand
Tel: +66 76 324 333
Fax: +66 76 324 100, 324 200
www.amanresorts.com
(See pages 84–87)

Babington House
Babington
Nr Frome
Somerset BA11 3RW
England
Tel: +44 1373 812 266
Fax: +44 1373 812 112
www.babingtonhouse.com
(The country house goes hip)

Ca'Pisani Hotel
Hotel Dorsoduro 979A
Venice 30123
Italy
Tel: +39 041 277 1478
Fax: +39 041 277 1061
www.capisanihotel.it
(A 16th-century palazzo with art deco furnishings)

Chateau de Bagnols
Bagnols 69620
France
Tel: +33 04 74 71 4000
Fax: +33 04 74 71 4049
www.bagnol.com
(Antique-laden interiors; a favourite with celebrities)

Chateau de Neiuil
Nieuil 16270
Charente
France
Tel: +33 05 45 71 36 38
Fax: +33 05 45 71 46 45
www. relaischateaux.com
(A former hunting palace of Francoisler)

The Delano
1685 Collins Avenue
Miami Beach, Florida 33139
USA
Tel: +1 305 672 2000
Fax: +1 305 532 0093
(A Philippe Starck-designed haven of purest white)

Devi Garh
P O Box No 144
Udaipur, 313001
Rajasthan
India
Tel: +91 2953-89211 to 20
Fax: +91 2953-89357
www.deviresorts.com
(See pages 5, 130, 131)

The Establishment
5 Bridge Lane, Sydney,
New South Wales 2000
Australia
Tel: +61 2 9240 3100
Fax: +61 2 9240 3101
www.luxehotels.com
(Glamour in an historic 19th-century building)

Hotel Byblos
Avenue Paul Signac
Saint-Tropez 83990
Tel: +33 04 94 56 68 00
Fax: +33 04 94 56 68 01
E-mail: saint-tropez@byblos.com
(Arabian Nights for jet-setters)

Hotel Explora
Sociedad Exploradora del Sur De America
Avda. Americo Vespucio Sur 80, Piso 5
Las Condes, Santiago de Chile
Tel: (56–2) 2066060
E-mail: explora@entelchile.net
(Situated at the foot of the Patagonia Mountains)

Hotel La Gazelle d'Or
Taroudannt 73000
Morocco
Tel: +212 885 2039
(Legendary destination hotel surrounded by orange
groves, with Moroccan interiors)

Hotel Meurice
228 Rue de Rivoli
Paris 75001
Tel: +33 1 44 58 10 10
Fax: +33 1 44 58 10 12
www.meuricehotel.com
(Steeped in history with 18th-century decor)

Hotel Nikko San Francisco
222 Mason Street
San Francisco
California 94102
USA
Tel: +1 415 394 1111
Fax: +1 415 421 0455
(Contemporary styling with a twist)

Hotel Triton
342 Gant Street
San Francisco
California
USA
Tel: 800 800 1299 (toll free)
Fax: +1 415 394 0555
www.hoteltriton.com
(West-coast whimsy for true originals)

Hotel im Wasserturm
Kaygasse 2
50676 Cologne
Germany
Tel: +49 221 200 80
Fax: +49 221 200 88
(Former 19th-century water tower with
modernist refurbishment)

Hudson Hotel
356 West 58th Street
New York, NY 10019
USA
Tel: +1 212 554 6000
Fax: +1 212 554 6001
www.hudsonhotel.com
(Hip hotel from Starck)

Jukkas AB
Marknadsvagen 63
S-981 91 Jukkasjärvi
Sweden
Tel: +46 980 66800
Fax: +46 980 66890
www.jukkas.se
(The extraordinary Ice Hotel)

The Kent Hotel
1131 Collins Avenue
Miami Beach, Florida 33139
USA
Tel: +1 305 604 5068
Fax: +1 305 531 0720.
(Barbara Hulanicki-designed refurbishment of
a classic art deco building)

The Mansion House Hotel
Werribee Park, K Road
Werribee, Victoria 3030
Australia
Tel: +61 3 9731 4000
Fax: +61 3 9731 4001
www.mansionhotel.com.au
(Cutting-edge aesthetics in a country house)

The Marlin Hotel
1200 Collins Avenue
Miami Beach, Florida 33139
Tel: +1 305 604 5063
Fax: +1 305 673 9609
(See pages 36–39)

Nilaya Hermitage Hotel
Arpora Bhati
Goa, 403518
India
Tel: +91 832 276793/94
Fax: +91 832 276792
www.nilayahermitage.com
(See pages 24–25)

Pavilion Hotel
346 Sussex Gardens
London W2 1UL
England
Tel: +44 020 7262 0905
Fax: +44 020 7262 1324
E-mail: pavilionlondon@aol.com
(Fantasy rooms for the connoisseur of the eclectic)

Portobello Hotel
22 Stanley Gardens
London W11 2NG
England
Tel: +44 020 7727 2777
Fax: +44 020 7792 9641
E-mail: info@portobello-hotel.co.uk
(For the eccentric bohemian)

Rajvilas Oberai Hotel
Goner Road,
Jaipur 303012
India
Tel: +91 141 680101
Fax: +91 141 680202
www.oberaihotels.com
(See pages 88–91)

Royalton Hotel
44 West 44th Street
New York 10036
USA
Tel: +1 212 869 4400
www.ianshragerhotels.com
(See pages 30–31)

Sanderson
50 Berners Street
London W1P 4AD
England
Tel: +44 020 7300 1400
Fax: +44 020 7300 1440
E-mail: reservation@sanderson.schragerhotels.com
(See pages 146–149)

Townhouse
150 20th Street
Miami Beach, Florida, 33139
USA
Tel: +1 305 534 3800
Fax: +1 305 534 3811
(Features a glow-in-the-dark water tower)

Umaid Bhawan Palace
Jodhpur 342 006
India
Tel: +91 291 510 101
Fax: +91 291 510 100
E-mail: ubp@ndf.vsnl.net.in
(See pages 78–79)

W Union Square
201 Park Avenue South
New York 10003
USA
Tel: +1 212 253 9119
Fax: +1 212 253 9099
www.whotels.com
(Slick, sleek sophistication)

RESTAURANTS

Blue Door
1685 Collins Avenue
Miami Beach, Florida 33139
USA
Tel: +1 305 674 6400
(Going-out as theatre, in the Delano Hotel)

Brasserie Bofinger
7 rue de la Bastille
Paris 75009
France
Tel +33 1 42 72 87 82
(The oldest brasserie in Paris with its original,
magnificent interior)

Fathom
11611 Ellison Wilson Road
Palm Beach Gardens, Florida
USA
Tel: +1 561 626 8788
www.fathomrestaurant.net
(Ocean views and light sculptures at each table)

Francouská Restaurace
Náměstí Republiky 5, Prague 1
Czech Republic
Tel: +4202 2 200 2777
(An exquisitely renovated shrine to art nouveau)

Hotel Europa Dining Room
1/7 Mikhailovskaya Ulitsa
St Petersburg
Russia
Tel: +7 812 329 6000
Fax: +7 812 329 6001
(A beautifully restored turn-of-the-century
dining room)

Hotel Metropole Dining Room
1/4 Teatralny Proyezd
Moscow 103012
Russia
Tel: +7 095 1209005
Fax: +7 095 7558858
(Russian art nouveau, with 3-storey dining room,
marble pillars and leaded-stained-glass roof)

The Park
118 Tenth Avenue
New York
USA
Tel: +1 212 352 3313
(The category-defying interior is described by its
management as "Palm Beach modernism,
chinoiserie chic, and down-home Zen")

Le Souk
47 Avenue B, between 3rd and 4th Streets
New York
USA
Tel: +1 212 777 5454
(Exotic North African-influenced interior)

The Red Sea Star Restaurant
Eilat, Israel
Tel: +972 634 7777
(A dreamy underwater restaurant submerged
20 feet below sea level)

Tao Bistro
42 East 58th Street
New York
USA
Tel: +1 212 888 2288
(Asian-influenced interior dominated by 16-foot
Buddha statue)

Le Train Bleu
Place Louis Armand
Gare de Lyon
Paris 75012
France
Tel: +33 01 43 43 09 06
Fax: +33 01 43 43 97 96
(Beautiful interior with columns and
painted ceilings)

BARS

Bar du Crillon
Hôtel du Crillon
16 Boissy d'Anglas
Paris 75008
France
Tel: +33 1 4471 1539
(Designed by the sculptor César in 1907 and
recently redecorated by Sonia Rykiel)

The Bar at The Marlin Hotel
1200 Collins Avenue
Miami Beach
Florida 33139
USA
Tel: +1 305 604 5052
Fax: +1 305 673 9609
(See pages 36–39)

China Club
50 rue de Charenton
Paris 75012
France
Tel: +33 1 4343 8202
(Speak-easy meets opium den)

Chinawhite
6 Air Street
London W1B 5AA
England
Tel: +44 020 7343 0040
www.chinawhite.com
(Louche orientalism for confirmed sybarites)

Claridge's Bar
Claridge's Hotel
Brook Street
London W1A 2JQ
England
Tel: +44 020 7629 8860
www.savoygroup.com
(Art deco bar designed by David Collins)

The Dresden Rooms
1760 N Vermont Avenue
Los Feliz, Los Angeles
California
USA
Tel: +1 323 665 4294
(Curved lines and white leather)

Hotel Costes Bar
239 rue St Honoré
Paris 75001
France
Tel: +33 1 4244 5000
www.hotelcostes.com
(Classic meets lounge lizard)

Light Bar
St Martins Lane Hotel
45 St Martins Lane
London WC2N 4HX
England
Tel: +44 020 7300 5500
(Philippe Starck-designed witty minimalism)

Pressure
110 University Place
New York
USA
Tel: +33 212 352 1161
(Futuristic glamour complete with inflated clouds)

Shu
Via Molino delle Armi
Milan 20100
Italy
Tel: +9 0258315720
(High-tech, futuristic glamour)

SHOPS

Basia Zarzycka
52 Sloane Square
London SW1W 8AX
England
Tel: +44 020 730 1660
Fax: +44 020 730 0065
E-mail:info@basia-zarzycka.co.uk
(Exquisitely beaded accessories and gowns)

Boutique Thierry Mugler
49 Av Montaigne
Paris 75008
France
Tel: +33 1 56 64 00 64
(Beautiful clothes, accessories, and perfumes)

Comme des Garçons
54 rue du Faubourg St Honoré
Paris 75008
France
Tel: +33 1 53 30 27 27
(An all-red interior, glossy as a lacquered box)

Lulu Guinness
3 Ellis Street
London SW1X 9AL
England
Tel: +44 020 7823 4828
Fax: +44 020 7823 4889
(A witty take on the glamour of the 1950s)

Jacqueline Morabito (Shop)
Boutique 3
3 rue Longchamp
Nice 06030
France
Tel/Fax: +33 4 93 88 35 00
(See home, pages 43–45)

Jacqueline Morabito (Studio)
42/44 rue Yves Klein
La Colle Sur Loup 06480
France
Tel: +33 4 93 32 64 92
Fax: +33 4 93 32 54 94
E-mail: jacqueline.morabito@libertysurf.fr

Moss
146 Greene Street
New York
USA
Tel: +1 212 226 2190
www.mossonline.com
(Cutting edge design for the home)

Prada Broadway
575 Broadway
New York
USA
Tel: +1 212 334 8888
(Shop with a high-tech interior)

Qiora Store & Spa
353 Madison Avenue
New York
USA
Tel: +1 212 527 9333
www.qiora.com
(Store-cum-spa with serene glass interior)

Seedhouse
487 West 22nd Street
New York
USA
Tel: +1 646 336 7333
(Eclectic fashion in a stunning shop;
by appointment only)

VV Rouleaux
54 Sloane Street
London SW1W 8AX
England
Tel: +44 020 7730 3125
(Ribbons, tassels, and trimmings for the indulgent)

PLACES
OF INTEREST

Galerie Beaubourg
Chateau Notre Dame des Fleurs
Vence 06140
France
Tel: +33 04 93 24 52 00
Fax: +33 04 93 24 52 19
www.galeriebeaubourg.com
(See pages 17–19)

Hearst Castle
San Simeon
Cambria, California
USA
Tel: +1 916 414 8400 ext. 4100
www.hearst-castle.org
(The media mogul's fantasy residence)

Leighton House
12 Holland Park Road
London W14 8LZ
England
Tel: +44 020 7602 3316
(Mosaic-decorated decadence)

Musée des Arts Décoratifs
Musée des Arts de la Mode et du Textile
Palais du Louvre
107 rue de Rivoli
Paris 75001
Tel: +33 1 44 55 57 50
Fax: +33 1 42 60 49 48
(A rich source of inspiration)

Palacio Real
Calle de Bailen
Madrid
Spain
Tel: +91 454 8700
(An extravagance on a grand scale)

Royal Pavilion
4-5 Pavilion Buildings
Brighton
East Sussex
BN1 1EE
England
Tel: +44 01273 292 822
Fax: +44 01273 292 821
www.royalpavilion.brighton.co.uk
(George IV's summer residence)

The Stencil Library
Stocksfield Hall,
Stocksfield, Northumberland,
NE43 7TN
England
Tel: +44 01661 844 844
Fax: +44 01661 843 984
E-mail: info@stencil-library.com
(See pages 40–41)

Versailles Palace
Place d'Armes
Versailles 78000
France
Tel: +33 1 30 84 74 00
www.chateauversailles.fr
(The residence of the Sun King)

The Vittoriale
via Vittoriale
Gardone Coast
Lake Garda
Tel: +39 0365 296 511
Fax: +39 0365 296 512
E-mail: info@vittoriale.it
(Gabriele D'Annunzio's celebration of the self)

INDEX

ACKNOWLEDGMENTS

THE AUTHORS

Without Deidi's beautiful pictures, Contemporary Glamour would never have come to life. Glamour also owes its gratitude to the inspiration, guidance, and assistance of Emma Clegg and Lara Maiklem, who brought the book's threads and its creators together in a seamless style. Without Auberon Hedgcoe and Emily Wilkinson's artful eye, this book would not look as striking as it does. And without editor Lindsay Porter, it would not read so elegantly. Glamour's authors would also like to thank their personal support team, Dan Turner and Paul Gillespie.

THE PHOTOGRAPHER

Deidi von Schaewen would like to thank all the owners of these glamorous places who have allowed her to enter into their lives and photograph their homes.
In England Jibby Beane, David and Claudia Dorell, Carolyn and Christian Hall, Kelly Hoppen, Mark Brazier-Jones, Rachel Morris, Matthew Williamson, Voon Wong.
In France Christian Astuguevieille, Armand Bartos, Didier Bohbot, Laurent Buttazoni, Pierre Cardin, Marianne and Pierre Nahon, Patrice and Magali Nourissat, Andrée Putman, Jeff Sayre, Pierre Staudenmeyer, Patrice Tatard.
In Germany Christian Duda and Carolin Heldmann, Erika Hoffmann, Paul Maenz.
In Tunisia Toni Facella Sensi.
In the USA John Barman, Michelle Oka Doner, Mandy and Cliff Einstein, Mary McFadden, James Goldstein, John Huggins, Wolfgang Joop, Karim Rashid, Hariett Selling, Betty Wasser.
In South Africa Pierre Lombard.
In India Lekha and Ranjan Poddar.

Many thanks to all the architects and designers who made these homes so glamorous:
Nicholas Antonopoulous and Charlie Deaton, Inni Chatterjee, Dowell & Benedetti, Souhed Ennemlaghi, Antti Lovag, Barbara Hulanicki, India Madhavi, Philippe Starck, Peter Shire, Claudio Silvestrin, Stefan Sterf, Ed Tuttle, Samir Wheaton.

Thanks also to all the glamorous hotels that opened their doors:
in London the Sanderson; in Morocco the Amanjena; in Thailand the Amanpuri; in India the Devi Garh, Nilaya Hermitage, Rajvilas, and Umaid Bhawan; in the USA the Marlin and the Royalton.

Speacial thanks to all the friends who have helped make this project possible and so very pleasant:
Alexandra d'Arnoux, Laurel Beizer, Marie Claire Blanckaerdt, Bruce Bonanto, Eileen and Larry Coyne, Jerome Dumoulin, Jodie Evans, Duggie Fields, Sigrid von Fischern, Patricia Foure, David Gill, Helena Heiss, Mira Hoefer, Ira Jaeger, Lisa Lovatt-Smith, Luise Mann, Ron Mann, Miralda, Ricardo Regazzoni, Jim and Colette Rossant, Dianne Dorren Sacks, July Saleström, Guido Stockmann, Pam Strayer, Natasha Struve, Angelika Taschen, Janet and Gerald Thomas, Rosario Uranja, Irene and Josi Vennekamp, Ralph Weiden.

And finally a big thank you to Ali Hanan and Kate Dwyer, who put glamour into beautiful words, and to the whole team at Mitchell Beazley, who made everything into a glamorous book, especially Emma Clegg, Lara Maiklem, Auberon Hedgecoe, and Emily Wilkinson.

PICTURE CREDIT

54/55/56/57 courtesy of Anoushka Hempel Design